FROM PRINCESS TO QUEEN

FROM PRINCESS TO QUEEN

SUMMER N DAWN

TRIGGER WARNINGS

If any of the following makes you feel unsafe or affects your mental health, please refrain from reading!

You and your mental health matter!

<u>Triggers:</u>
SEX
ABUSE
VIOLENCE
PAST ABUSE
PREGNANCY
STALKING

TO ASH, NEVER FORGET HOW STRONG YOU ARE! THANK YOU FOR BEING THERE THROUGH IT ALL! I LOVE YOU FOREVER AND ALWAYS! I CAN'T WAIT TO SEE WHAT MEMORIES WE MAKE TOGETHER!

TO MY BOOK BESTIES, YOU ALWAYS KEEP ME GOING AND NEVER LET ME GIVE UP! I APPRECIATE YOU MORE THAN YOU KNOW! YOUR LIVES ARE GOING TO BE EVERYTHING YOU HAVE EVER DREAMED OF!

TO SUNSHINE, YOU SUPPORT ME THROUGH IT ALL EXCEPT BY READING MY BOOKS, BUT I LOVE YOU ANYWAY!

Playlist

All rights to these songs are the property of their respective owners; I do not own the rights to any of them!

These songs are here to enhance your reading experience and trigger your emotions.

Hailey's Playlist:

(These songs are not in order. Some songs will be listed at the beginning of the chapter.)

Bad Romance by Lady Gaga

Love Myself by Hailee Steinfeld

This is Me (from Camp Rock) by Demi Lovato and Joe Jonas

I Am Not Okay by Jelly Roll

Fly on The Wall by Miley Cyrus

Confident by Demi Lovato

Made in The USA by Demi Lovato

Its OK Not to Be OK by Marshmello and Demi Lovato

VIII ~ TRIGGER WARNINGS

Enter....

Enter a world that allows every Princess to spread their wings and grow into their crown.

Sometimes, it takes a mysterious man to bring out the Princess's freaky side.

Then, other times, it takes a mask and a sex club!

WILL YOU....

ENTER MY DUNGEON WITH CAUTION...

XII ~ TRIGGER WARNINGS

1

Prologue

Dark.

Demented.

Naked.

The screams.

The smell of urine and vomit.

The dust and mold in the air.

The constant dripping of water in the corner.

His hands snaked down my body.

They were firm, never gentle.

He always wore a mask and always whispered.

The one phrase that stuck with me keeps replaying over and over and over again.

"You're a princess who must earn her crown. You have been handed everything by your brother; it's time you come into your own."

I will come into my own!

That's why I came here.

I needed a break from my brother's watchful eye.

Kass helped me, and here I am in the dungeon at Kastaways.

I'm safe.

But I will find who I am without having to watch every step I take.

Let the exploration begin.

2

Sibling Tension

H^{*ailey*}

Three months ago....

You have got to be fucking kidding me?

Massimo sent me home from work again.

He claims that there's nothing to be concerned with for the next few weeks.

I will find out the truth; Kass keeps me in the loop.

I couldn't ask for a better sister-in-law, but she put my big brother in his place.

I head up to their apartment, and I hear the Phantom of the Opera soundtrack playing.

Kass loves her musicals, especially HSM.

I use my key card to get in.

Massimo said I'm only supposed to use it for emergencies, but whenever he's not home, I use it to hang with Kass.

Kass keeps me sane, especially when my brother drives me crazy!

Kass is in the kitchen baking brownies; she doesn't know how to relax.

She is always doing something, if she's not cooking then she's cleaning.

If she's cleaning she's crafting with the babies.

Kass keeps Roe and Asia's little girl when Asia has to work.

Big brother makes sure Asia doesn't have to work often because he knows how much she loves spending time with her baby.

Kass sees me and treats me like the strong woman I am, not like Massimo.

Massimo treats me like a porcelain doll. He would rather keep me on a shelf than use my talents for the good of the Bratva.

I'm one of the best snipers in the entire Bratva, but he only lets me use my skills when he seems it necessary.

My kill count is one; that's it.

How will people fear me if I can't use what I'm good at?

Kass sees me, "What did he do now?"

I sit at the counter and sigh, "He sent me home because he says there's nothing he needs me to do right now. This is the third time this week!"

Kass looks at me and replies, "You know things are safe right now? They haven't had to work in a while on the non-legal side. They have just been taking clients with the legal business. I'm sure he's not trying to push you away. Maybe he's just trying to give you a break. He knows how hard you work."

I stared at the table.

"Kass I'm tired of him treating me like I'm breakable. I want to help with the business and be a part of his inner circle. It's like he doesn't want me to do that. It's like nothing I do for him is good enough."

Kass comes over and rubs my back, "Love, he's protecting you. He told me your story, he never wants anything like that to happen again. You, me, and the Bratva is all he has control of; he can't stand to lose you. But do you just want more freedom?"

Of course he told Kass what happened with my dad!

I look at Kass, all I see is compassion in her eyes.

"Kass, I want freedom so bad it hurts! But Kass, I have to tell you something, and you have to swear not to tell Massimo! You pinky swear?"

She scrunches her brows and holds out her pinky, "Hailey, you know I hate keeping secrets from him! But because it's you, I will do it."

She pinky promises.

I take a deep breath.

"Kass, I have not dated anybody ever. You know, Massimo watches me like a hawk. I've never had a boyfriend, and I've never had a first kiss."

Kass is shocked, but the compassion is still radiating from her eyes and pores.

"Hailey, do you feel like you're ready to explore your love life?"

Kass is staring deep into my soul.

I swallow, "Yes! I want to know what love or lust is like! But I can't do that with Massimo micromanaging my every move! I want to have a choice! I want happiness. I don't want to be a princess. I want to be somebody's queen!"

Kass smirked, "I will cover for you. But you're going to have to work for me from now on, deal?"

I look at Kass with a renewed sense of fire, "Deal!"

She giggles, "Great! You leave tomorrow early in the morning. I'm booking you a flight so Massimo doesn't ask any questions. Jared will drive you. Be ready at 3:30 am. You will find what you are looking for, but you will do me a favor, too."

3

Managing Kastaways

P*resent Day...*

Dorian

When Massimo sent me away, I didn't think it would be to run his wife's club.

Here I am in Gulfport, Mississippi, running Kastaways.

Everything on the crime front in Chicago has slowed down ever since we ended the sex trafficking ring.

Massimo asked me if I would come down here to ensure the efficient operation of Kass's new club.

They also gave me 25% of the club just for running it.

I didn't want it, but Massimo and Kass both insisted.

Massimo takes care of all of us in the Bratva.

He may be my boss, but he is my best friend and brother.

He has been there for me through everything, including the death of my mother when I was just a child.

No matter what, I'll always be by his side.

My loyalty to him will never wane.

He could ask me to do anything, and I would do it.

With all my training, I never thought I would run a nightclub.

But not just any nightclub, a nightclub with a hidden underground sex club.

Who would have thought that sweet little Kass would develop this idea?

All of us in the Bratva know that Kass is a badass who knew she had kinks.

But that is none of my business, but apparently this club is now partly my business.

I have been here in Gulfport for almost a year now.

Kass ran everything when it first opened, and it worked like a well-oiled machine.

I want to keep it up to her standards.

Kass was very picky with her hiring process.

Only people who could pass the Bratva initiation test can work at Kastaways.

She wanted strong but discreet people because of the underground club.

I have used the amenities of the club; I like to watch.

If they had women I was interested in, then maybe I would participate in the scenes.

When I'm not working upstairs, I'm actually overseeing the secret part of the underground club.

We call it the dungeon; it's a bare room that we use for intense sex training.

Only a few women have made it through the three-week training.

Usually Paul does the training, and I oversee everything.

But Paul said one of Kass's handpicked employees has decided that she wants to join the dungeon training.

I have not met her yet because she has been working upstairs with Toree training at the bar.

Paul described her to me.

He said she's 5 foot 4 inches tall with brown hair and gets lost in their blue eyes.

Sounded to me like Paul is crushing on the new girl.

I'll let Paul have his fun as long as it doesn't get out of hand.

He said she's been working here for 3 months, and Toree said the new girl has been busting her ass at the bar.

Toree also said most of the men who come into the club have tried to get her to go to the underground with them.

But she just declines with a smile and goes back to work.

Kass texted me when the new girl started and told me to ensure Toree takes good care of her.

I found this weird.

I know Kass cares about all of her employees, but I felt that it was more of a threat than guidance.

Paul said he would start her training tonight after her swift, but he said he would take it slow because he has a feeling she's new to the sex club world.

We don't get many newbies here.

Most of our clientele is rich and highly trained in the kinky world of sexual interaction.

I will definitely be interested in overseeing this training if it is true.

Kastaways can bring the farthest gone outcast into the light.

4

Training Introduction

Hailey

I never thought working my ass off would bring me joy.

I love my job.

I might be a bartender and server, but I'm free to do what I please without my big brother micromanaging my every step.

Toree has trained me well, and she is super sweet.

Toree knows how to run the bar without making any mistakes; she must be the manager's right hand.

I still have not gotten the chance to meet the manager, I have met Paul but he's the "special" trainer.

When Kass told me she opened a club with a twist, I was not expecting the twist to be two underground sex clubs!

She doesn't hold back when you ask her to do something; I just wanted maybe a few sexual escapades!

Instead, she sends me to work in a hidden sex club!

Ok, let's be honest....

I'm not complaining!

I will definitely be able to discover myself here!

Which is why I signed up for what Toree called the "intense training camp."

She said only a few people have made it through the whole program.

Paul runs the training program, but Toree said you can't be shy because they have the manager overseeing the program.

Apparently, he can see you, but you can see him.

Tonight, my training starts as soon as I clock out.

Paul said he would meet me right here at the bar.

He said that tonight, he would just be exploring and learning the ropes.

I just have to get through these next four hours, and then I hope the fun begins.

Four hours and five minutes later......

Tonight was slammed!

I served over three hundred drinks tonight!

The tips were so good!

In my last four hours of work, I made $350 in tips!

But it's not all about money for me; it's about freedom from my big brother.

I haven't been kissed or even caressed by a man.

Yes, I have had wet dreams.

Yes, I have touched myself.

Yes, I have a vibrating boyfriend.

I've done sexual things to myself, but my purity is intact.

I have had fantasies about who I would give it to, but I would rather not have their death on my hands.

Paul comes up to me and kisses me on the cheek.

Oh boy!

I'm automatically flustered!

"Good evening, Hailey! I hope you had a good shift. Are you ready for the tour?" Paul says as he asses my body.

I swallow, "Yes, sir! Ripe and ready!"

Why the fuck did I just say that?!

Paul just smirked and whispered, "Baby girl, your innocence leaks out of your pores."

Umm, excuse the fuck out of me?!

"Paul, be careful. I may be innocent when it comes to this club world. But I have seen, and done more than you have. How long of you been with the Bratva?"

You can feel Paul's wonder and excitement.

"Little girl, I bet you know nothing of the Ballentine Bratva. They are not from these parts. I don't have to answer to you, " he remarked.

This cocky asshole.

It's a good thing I retrieved my phone from my locker.

"Hold that thought, Paul." I whipped out my phone, I know Kass only gave my first name but I will stand for no disrespect.

Kass picks up on the first ring, "Hey Hey, what's up girlie? How's work going?"

"Hey Kass, can you please explain to Paul here who works for you. That I'm not a fragile little being, and that I've been around the Bratva since it was formed?"

Kass screams, almost bursting my eardrum, "YOU HAVE TO BE FUCKING JOKING." She takes a deep breath and responds with her boss' voice, "Put Paul Ruiz on the phone now!"

I looked at Paul. "Kass wants to talk to you. You better answer her before she goes to get her husband."

I hand him the phone and his face drops.

Paul keeps trying to get a word in.

"Ma'am I didn't..."

"No, I respect you, but it's.."

"I don't answer to women!"

Oh shit!

Of course, that would be the only full sentence she would let him get out that would offend her.

"Ma'am, no, I'm sorry! Please don't tell him! I will do anything!"

There was a slight pause, and he replied, "Yes, ma'am. I'll give her a tour, and I'll hand her over."

He hands the phone back to me.

He won't look at me.

"Kass, what did you say to him?" I say to her.

"He knows where he fucked up. He has to deal with his manager. He will give you the tour. He has not to touch you or to even make any other comments to you. He can only answer your questions. He will be punished, nobody will disrespect you, and I mean, nobody. Paul knows who you are now, he will not be doing your training. Yes, I know you signed up for the dirty course. No judgment here. I will assign someone else to you. Be safe and have fun, love you hey hey!"

Well damn, Kass took that to heart, "I love you too, Kass! Thank you."

I look at Paul, "Ready to give me that tour, Mr. Ruiz?"

He finally looks at me, "I am so sorry!" He whispers, "I didn't know you were Mr. Ballentine's sister. I will mind my tongue and hands for as long as I have them. Let's give you that tour."

Well, I'll be damn some manners!

I nod at him.

He takes me to the VIP elevator.

"This will take you to the first level of the underground club. Once we navigate through there, I will show you the dungeon. Then, you will be free to explore only the first level tonight. You are not allowed in the dungeon without being let in and the master is there. We will glance at level one, then I'll show you the dungeon and bring you back here to roam."

I nod, "Thank you, Mr. Ruiz."

The elevator doors open.

Paul replies, "This is what Kass calls the Kast Lounge. You have everything from a stage where you can watch couples play and private booths that's can make invisible or let people watch. There is also themed rooms here that are sound proof, but you are given a safety device before entering."

This underground is huge!

The main floor is basically a big orgie area or arena, I should say.

As we kept walking, Paul opened one of the themed rooms.

This one happens to be a normal-looking office room,

There is a big oak desk and a throne chair, bookshelves lining the walls, and a big sofa in the middle.

I wonder what kind of sex scenes could happen there?

Paul leads us to the final elevator, "When we get down here, we have to be quiet. The dungeon master is going to be playing with one of his playthings. He knows we are coming, but you will go straight into the observation room. I am to assist him."

Well damn, get a show on the first night!

The elevator slides into position, and Paul gets out first.

Paul has a finger to his lips and leads me into the observation room.

There's a blue leather couch and a satin swing in the observation room.

Paul whispers, "Here's the panic button if you need it. It's a one-way glass, so you will be able to hear and see us, but we can't see and hear you. The master will go over the rules for your benefit, so pay attention."

I let out the breath I was holding, "Thank you, Mr. Ruiz."

Paul locks me in the observation room.

My eyes darted to the dungeon.

The dungeon is aptly named, and it's as bare as they can get.

There is a mattress on the floor and a Saint Andrew's cross in the corner.

I can hear the constant dripping of water, but I can see where it is coming from.

Paul enters first.

He is shirtless, and a red heart tattoo is on his left pectoral muscle.

My brother has one, too, but he has a crown on it because this is their Bratva tattoo, and he is the leader or king.

My brother had everyone get one, and they had the joining date on the bottom right corner of the heart.

I can't make out the date of Paul's.

I have one, too; mine is on my hip bone.

Mine doesn't have a date; it's like Massimo's; it has an infinity sign instead of a date.

Paul speaks, "I, Paul Ruiz, repent for my crimes against the Ballentine Bratva. I will take whatever punishment the Master has for me. I acknowledge that Queen Kassani has set my punishment in the hands of the Prince and Master. I am sorry for my crimes; do what you must master."

Umm... what the fuck is happening here?!

5

Master

It's OK Not to Be OK by Marshmello and Demi Lovato

Dorian

He fucking touched her!

Paul touched the Princess of the Bratva!

He touched Hailey, and he disrespected her.

What the hell is wrong with him?

Now, she will see me punish Paul while learning the rules.

Paul will receive ten whips with my new whip while reciting the dungeon rules.

I opted to take a few precautions so that Hailey wouldn't recognize me for a while.

I will not use my sharp demanding voice that's easily recognizable, I will use my sexy and distinctive whisper.

The dungeon's acoustics are lovely; even a whisper can be heard on the other side of the room.

Also, I opted for a Phantom mask; Kass was kind enough to give me one from her collection.

I know I haunt the women who wish they could stay under my rule.

I covered my Bratva date with scar tape; if she sees my infinity symbol, she will know.

Massimo wanted me to know I am as important as him and Hailey.

Only four of us have an infinity symbol with our hearts, the fourth is Marcus.

Our bond will never be broken.

My heart is located on my right shoulder.

When Kass called me earlier, I knew what I needed to do.

I need to see if this is what she really wants or if she is a regular-sex girl.

Kass has entrusted me with Hailey.

I know Massimo told her he can't hide anything from his wife.

I have wanted Hailey for myself for years.

She is strong and fragile at the same time.

She knows what she wants and when she wants it.

Hailey is the reason I took the job here in Gulfport.

Massimo was noticing my attachment to Hailey.

He looks at me like family, but nobody is good enough for the Princess of the Ballentine Bratva, not even the Prince or Master.

Here, I'm known as the Master; no one dares to disobey me.

Back in Chicago, I'm known as the Prince of the Ballentine Bratva because Massimo claims me as his Capo.

There are nights when I am here in the dungeon, and I have a woman or two doing anything I ask, but I can't get off.

There are so many nights where I have had to take my pleasure into my own hands.

There's only one thing that can get me to the point of no return.

HAILEY.

Kass asked me to help her on her journey, so I will do that.

I'll make Hailey the queen of the bedroom.

Or if she wants, she can be my Queen, the queen of my blue heart.

I have been blue since 2019.

No woman will stay with me, the sad prince.

The prince who is always pining for the princess.

It's a good thing my face is hidden.

After she sees what I'm about to do to Paul, she may not want to come near me.

That's a risk I have to take.

Kass ordered his punishment, and I refuse to get on her bad side.

I enter the dungeon with a mask on my face and a chest bare.

I disguise my whisper, "Paul, kneel. You know why you are being punished today. State the reason."

Paul swallows, "I am being punished for offending and touching the Bratva Princess. I broke the golden rule, which states that consent is always to be given. I also broke rule number two: do not touch anyone who belongs to Kass or master."

"Thank you, Paul. Now that you understand why you're being punished, we will begin. You will recite all the rules to the Princess while you receive ten lashes with the whip. That is just your first punishment; then, we will continue after that is complete. Are you ready?"

Paul sighs, "Yes, Master. Number one, consent is always required."

Before Paul could even get the word required out, the whip slashes his back with full force.

He crumpled to the ground but automatically snapped back up with obedience.

"Number two, do not touch anyone who belongs to Kass or Master without the proper permission."

SMACK

"Fuck! Number three, always be on your knees in the dungeon unless told otherwise."

SMACK

"I am sorry, Master. Number four, all outer clothing is to be left in the observation room unless instructed otherwise."

SMACK

Paul is hysterically crying now.

"Number five, Master, is always to be obeyed."

SMACK

"Number six, always have a safe word."

SMACK

"Number seven, no lying to the Master."

SMACK

"Number eight, emotions are meant to be expressed; never hide them."

SMACK

Paul crumpled again but had a slow recovery this time.

I'm using full force just like he deserves.

Hailey is mine.

"Number nine what happens in the dungeon stays in the dungeon."

SMACK

"Number ten, never regret your actions, only own them and accept all consequences."

SMACK

Paul crumples to the floor.

"Thank you, Master. I own my actions and accept all consequences."

I lift Paul off the ground.

I hit the button on the wall to unlock the observation room.

"Princess, come here. Follow the arrows on the floor. You will decide Paul's second punishment."

6

The Master's Princess

Fly on the Wall by Miley Cyrus

Hailey

The door automatically flings open.

Master wants me to decide Paul's subsequent punishment.

So, I'm getting a chance to play tonight!

This situation has taken an unexpected turn.

I slowly exit the observation room.

If only people could see what goes on down here.

What should I do when I get in there?

I will kneel.

As I enter the dungeon, my body has a natural reaction.

I sink to my knees on the cold, hard floor, my heart racing as a torrent of words spills from my lips, spilling forth before I can fully grasp their meaning.

"Thank you for the invitation, Master. How can I be of service?"

I keep my eyes on the floor until he gives me directions.

He whispered, "Rise. You may look at me."

My eyes slowly rise up his luscious body.

His physique looks like it was ripped right off a romance novel cover!

I can't help but marvel at his sculpted muscles, powerful legs that exude strength, and chiseled chin that gives him an air of confident charm.

Those captivating eyes hold a magnetic allure that draws me in.

His image is etched in my mind, and it is a delightful fantasy I can revisit anytime.

I can't help but wonder just what those strong arms are capable of!

He speaks slowly, "Princess, Paul has two options for his final punishment. You're the judge and jury. Should he take his last breath right here, right now? Or should we deny him pleasure and make him watch us explore each other? Your choice, princess."

He wants me to choose between Paul's death or denying him pleasure?!

How fucked up is this guy?

I look at Paul; he looks scared shitless.

Paul notices me and repeats, "I have accepted all consequences and punishments."

I look back at the floor, "Master, I don't want Paul to die. I feel he has learned his lesson. But I'm not ready for an audience."

Master whispers, "Why is that, princess?"

I let out a soft sigh, feeling the weight of my words. "This princess has been trapped in a cage for far too long. She embodies purity and innocence, untouched by the darkness of the outside world."

7

Clarity

Love Myself by Hailee Steinfeld

Dorian

That old English was a turn-on.

She's a virgin?

Holy shit!

This is every master's fantasy!

This is my fantasy, one I didn't see coming true.

Pull yourself together!

I clear my throat.

"Paul, leave us. The princess has spared you. Remember, no one needs to know her identity."

Paul replies, "Yes, Master. The princess's secret is safe with me."

As Paul steps out of the dimly lit dungeon, he strives to carry himself with as much dignity as he can muster, despite the weight of the darkness lingering in his thoughts.

Hailey stands nearby, a chill running down her spine as the cool air brushes against her skin.

Let's see what we can find out.

"Don't be afraid, princess. I'm here to teach you, to guide you. Where in the world have you been hiding?"

I love her giggle, "Quoting Phantom song lines? Very corny."

"What sweet seduction lies before us?"

Her laughter fills the air, a light and infectious sound that only grows louder.

"You've spent too much time with Kass," she teases, a playful glint in her eyes.

"Have you been in the breakroom lately? It feels like she's manipulating the speakers from Chicago!" I reply, shaking my head in disbelief at the absurdity of it all.

Hailey throws her head back, her entire body shaking with laughter as she leans forward, nearly collapsing with the joy of the moment.

After finally catching her breath, she gazes into my eyes with a hint of vulnerability and says, "It feels like I've known you for ages. Being with you gives me an overwhelming sense of safety. Is that strange?"

The words hang in the air, heavy with the warmth of our connection.

I smirk, "I am free from the prison of my mind."

8

Confident

Confident by Demi Lovato

Hailey

His puns are not lost on me.

I have some of my own.

But I will save them for now.

He leans in closer, his voice barely above a whisper as he asks, "Tell me, princess, what makes you so pure?"

What a dumb question!

"How new are you? You know who I am, and you're clearly buddy buddy with Kass. I am as pure as snow because of my knight in shining armor! The one that always protects my virtue at all costs, the one that will kill any man who looks in my direction! Your boss, my big brother! Who has no idea I am doing this because Kass covered for me."

Master caresses my cheek with the back of his hand, "I am not scared, princess. I am the big bad wolf."

Well, there goes my panties!

I swallow, "I can't wait to be your student."

He yanks my head back, grasping my hair by the root.

He breathes in my scent. "This training will be different from any other training before. You might just need to be mine, princess."

Umm....yes, please boss me around!

9

Naked but NOT Afraid

Bad Romance by Lady Gaga

Dorian

TWO WEEKS LATER..

We have been stretched thin with the influx of people these two weeks.

This is the first time the princess and I are getting to play.

Tonight, the dungeon smells of vomit, and you can hear the screams of pleasure from above.

Hailey is naked, willing, and full of fire.

"You're a princess who must earn her crown. Your brother has handed you everything; it's time you come into your own."

She responds obediently, "Yes, Master. I will earn it!"

I unhook her from the cross.

"You are ready to earn your crown. Get dressed, princess. We are heading upstairs to the second level. You're too pure for this training."

Hailey looks at me with those sad but curious eyes.

" I trust you, master. But this better be fun. I've been waiting for a taste of what you offer for weeks. If you make me wait any longer, I may just have to take things into my own hands."

Oh, the little devil.

Little does she know I have been taking matters into my own hands every night.

Her face.

Her curves.

The way she carries herself.

Her feisty attitude.

Those perky breasts.

Seeing her naked today will be forever ingrained in my mind.

She walks into the observation room to get dressed; I turn away from her so I can itch my face.

The mask irritates me, especially when I sweat.

10

Clothed but Tempted

*H**ailey*

As I get dressed in the observation room, I see him turn away.

He looks like he is scratching or rubbing his face.

Why does he wear the mask?

What does he have to hide?

A man like him should not hide who he is.

He looks like a gift from the devil himself, the kind that's made with black magic.

Addicting, once you get a taste, you can't stop.

That's how my body feels, I never want his hands to leave my body.

He thinks I'm too pure for his training.

I'm going to have to crank up the fire a little bit.

Let's see what he plans on level two.

Am I scared?

No.

Am I excited?

To the core!

Master doesn't know it yet, but he's awakening feelings that I didn't know I was hiding.

I hope he's used to playing with fire.

If not, he may just get burned.

This little virgin is not backing down.

I will find out his true identity, but until then, I will have some fun.

Before we exit the dungeon, Master stops me.

"Princess, you will take the elevator to the second level and mingle. Watch the show, and we will discuss it later. Be ready. I am sending you someone to meet with tonight. Treat him respectfully; I know he knows you and your brother."

A test?

Game on!

"Yes, Master."

Excitement pulses through my veins.

Who could Master be sending me?

What does tonight hold?

The elevator takes its sweet time getting to the second level.

The club is in full swing tonight.

The stage is empty, but people are reserving their cubicles for the show.

Fortunately, the bar's atmosphere is pleasantly calm, a welcome change from the usual hustle and bustle.

As I scan the room, I spot my favorite bartender behind the counter, expertly mixing drinks and serving patrons, having taken a shift in this cozy establishment.

It feels reassuring to see a familiar face, adding a touch of warmth to the serene setting.

A setting that is about to be set on fire when the show starts; Toree has told me stories.

"Hey, sexy lady, are you working hard or hardly working?"

Toree smiles, "Hardly working! Fancy seeing you here. How's the training going?"

I sigh, "It's going. The Master thinks I am too pure, and he's trying a different approach. But honestly, I just want to fuck somebody at this point!"

Toree snorts, "Desperate much?"

"Haha, very funny." I lower my voice to a whisper, "I'm just tired of being a virgin. If someone from my past walked through that door, I would probably jump their bones!"

Toree looked behind me, "Well, I think you spoke your wish into existence."

I slowly turn around.

Sauntering towards me is the man of my fantasies, the man that was only replaced by my Master recently.

Dorian Petrov.

"Well fuck me!"

Toree giggles, "He just might!"

11

Fooling the Princess

D^{*orian*}

I will not let her figure out that I'm the Master.

Right now, I'm just Dorian, the annoying Capo.

She has a look of horror and embarrassment on her face.

Good.

She needs to channel that, or rather, we need to channel it.

I will push her to her limits as just me and not as the phantom.

I want her.

I crave her.

My hands are itching to touch her.

I want to light her fire!

I want us to burn together.

12

To Smash or To Pass

H^{*ailey*}

"Toree, hush!"

She just keeps giggling until Dorian reaches the bar.

"Good evening, Dorian. What can I get you?"

Thank you Toree!

I really don't think I can form words right now.

Dorian replies, "Just whiskey on the rocks, please, Tore."

He turns his wandering eyes my way.

He takes in my attire, I probably look like I got run over by an eighteen wheeler.

Master had me sweating and squirming!

Master made me scream with just his fingers!

Master is not here.

Is Dorian who Master sent me?

Dorian demands, "Why are you here, Hailey? Gulfport is no place for you. You need to be back in Chicago. I am sure many of the women need you."

Um, rude.

"Kass made sure all the women could contact me if they needed to, it's called a cellphone. Have you heard of it? Any place can be for me! I work here, so I can play here too. You're not the boss of me. What are you doing here anyway? Massimo said you were on a long assignment."

Dorian downs his whiskey, "Yes, I am on an assignment. I can't tell you details right now, but for some reason Kass asked me to drop in here and keep an eye on things for a while. She has a few concerns about some of the employees. But I meant why are you on this level? You should be up top."

I snap, "And you should've said goodbye when you left Chicago a year and a half ago!"

Oops, that wasn't supposed to come out.

"Awe. Were you mad at me, sugar? Did you actually miss me?"

Shit!

Time to backtrack.

"I don't know what you're talking about, Crazy Capo. What brings you here tonight besides watching the employees? You can watch me anytime."

Damn it!

Why did I say that?

Why am I flirting with him?

I have had no alcohol today, but I have lost my damn mind!

He smirks, "I can watch you anytime. What can I watch you do? Do you think you can handle my eyes roaming all over your curvy body?"

He has actually looked at my body?

Roaming?

How would he describe me?

Is this the same Crazy Capo that used to annoy the shit out of me?

Could he be dreaming of me like I was dreaming of him?

Should I smash him?

Master said to treat the guest with respect, would it be respectful to fulfill my fantasies with this Capo?

Should I worry about what Big Brother would think?

Nope!

Big Brother has nothing to do with this!

What about Master?

Master has dragged this out too damn long!

I accept all punishment and consequences.

Time to be confident.

Time to regret nothing.

Time to live out my sex fantasy.

Time to let this Capo deflower me.

Time to straighten my crown.

Time to smash.

13

My Fantasy Comes True

D^{orian}

I see the wonder in her eyes.

She has been the main star of my fantasies for over five years.

HER EYES.

HER HAIR.

HER LIPS.

HER LEGS.

They may be short, but those legs make me want to feel them up 24/7!

HER ASS.

If I could stare at it all day, I would.

HER VOLUPTUOUS CHEST.

I was never a breast guy until Hailey.

I want to put my face in them or use them as a pillow.

HER ATTITUDE.

"So, Crazy Capo, are you here to play tonight? Or are you here to stalk?" Hailey purrs.

She is openly flirting with me!

Seems like my dreams may come true tonight!

Yes, I've seen her naked as Master, but she has no idea.

I have spanked her and even fingered her.

But I would do anything to have her as just Dorian or even as her Crazy Capo.

Let's see where we can take this.

"I might play if I can find someone willing. I have a certain type I go for."

Her brow scrunches, "What type do you go for, Crazy Capo?"

There she goes with that nickname again!

She came up with that nickname when I snatched her gun from her to save her life.

Ever since then, she has called me Crazy Capo.

She wasn't scared that I killed him; she was shocked that I effortlessly snatched her gun from her with no effort.

I really am crazy about the Ballentine Princess.

"My type is mouthy, curvy, and willing."

With long brown hair and the sweetest eyes.

"So basically any women walking and talking.," She huffs.

"No, sugar. I have someone specific in mind."

She looks at me quizzically, "Who would that be, Crazy Capo?"

I smirk, "I have known her for years. She is very mouthy. Her favorite color is black. She would rather have long hair than short hair. She finds hot water more relaxing than cold. She can kill someone in ten seconds or less. She likes helping women in need. She doesn't realize how attractive she is. She sways her hips as she walks to let everyone know she's in charge. Her eyes pull you in, and they won't let you go until she says so. She may look fragile, but she hasn't been fragile for a long time. She needs to be more confident, but I think I can bring it out of her. But most of all I want her to be mine."

She swallows, "Where do you find a girl like that? How did you find out so much about her?"

"I have been watching her for years. She thinks I am crazy, but little does she know I am crazy for her."

She shifts in her seat, "Who is she, Crazy Capo? She sounds like a lucky lady."

She really doesn't see her worth.

"Her initials are H.B. Does that ring any bells?"

There it is!

The fire ignites in her eyes!

She scoots closer to me and slides her palm up and down on my leg.

My eyes were so focused on her caressing me that I didn't notice her face coming closer to mine.

"I consent to everything. I will be yours, Crazy Capo."

She grabs my hair and thrusts her lips against mine.

Well fuck!

She tastes like sugar.

Her lips are as soft as velvet.

She is kissing me like she is craving me, like she needs me.

I am royally screwed.

14

Purity, Say GOODBYE

H^{AILEY}

I feel the whiskey on his tongue.

His lips were made for me.

Never would I have guessed that he knew so much about me.

He knows things that Massimo doesn't even know.

This virgin is saying goodbye to her purity!

I kiss his ear, "Take me to the office playroom. Show me how crazy you can be."

He growls, "Your wish is my command, sugar!"

Toree mouths, "I want all the damn details!"

As I shake my head, Dorian is dragging to the playroom I suggested.

He pays the guard standing outside the playroom.

The guard addresses me, "Here is your safety device, ma'am. Just hit that button, and someone will come to your aid. Enjoy."

I just nod as Dorian pulls me in and locks the door.

"Are you sure about this, sugar?"

I blink at him, "I fully consent. Do you consent to taking my virginity?"

He looks momentarily shocked, "Only if you are ready to be mine."

I smirk, "Come what may, I will be yours, Capo!"

He growls and pushes me up against the desk, "No turning back now, sugar."

I pull on his shirt to drag him to me, "No regrets, Capo. Make me yours, now!"

"Wish granted!"

Fuck!

There is no better feeling than his lips on my neck!

15

Outsider Looking In

G^{host}

The office playroom, really?

Who would have fun in there?

She is a virgin?!

He should not be the one to take her virginity.

He wouldn't treat her like I would.

I have been hiding in the shadows since she was born.

I have watched Hailey grow into the Princess she is today.

Now, I am standing outside Kastaways watching the feed from the playroom on my burner phone.

Paul called me in to fix a security camera issue, while i was there I tapped into the firewall so I could watch Hailey.

She should be mine.

I purchased her fair and square from her father!

His dumbass got caught and killed!

I want what I deserve!

HAILEY!

I am going to watch and see how he fucks her; I vow to do it better!

The Princess will be my slave!

I watch and listen carefully.

"Sugar, take off your clothes. Nice and slow, baby."

BARF!

Slow?!

No, thank you!

Fast and furious.

Well, then again, Hailey looks sexy and moves slowly.

She is swaying her hips as she removes her tights and then her skirt.

It makes my mouth water and my pants tight.

It's a good thing the signal will reach my car; I have a feeling I'm going to need some privacy.

It's also good that my windows are tinted as dark as they go.

There she stands, unbuttoning her shirt.

Those breasts could knock someone out, and I am sure no one would complain!

Hailey looks at him with angel eyes; you can see the devotion in her eyes.

That should be me!

"Take me, Capo! Stop making me wait! Turn me around, bend me over this desk, and fuck me like the naughty girl you know I am!"

Well, damn!

Hailey is not a little girl anymore.

She's a mouthy woman.

I can't wait to see what that mouth can do.

"Command me, sugar! I will grant all your wishes!"

He swings her around and rips her panties off of her.

He slides his finger into her.

He bites her ear, "Ride my fingers. I have to get you ready for me, baby. Do you want me hard and fast, or do you want me soft and sensual? Tell me, baby. I'm here for you."

BARF!

Hailey moans, "Crazy Capo, take me! Take my purity! You better not be slow! You take me how you need me! Let's ride this together! Like you said, I haven't been fragile for a long time. So i want my toes curling and juices dripping down my legs!"

The little girl knows how to talk dirty!

I set my dick free and stroke it as they continue.

"Anything for you, Angel! Get ready. It will only hurt for a second. You are soaked, I love that this is for me!"

It will be for me soon.

I stroke it harder and faster; her panting is getting to me.

"IF YOU DON'T GET INSIDE ME RIGHT..."

Hailey can't even finish her sentence.

Dorian pounds himself into her.

"Take me, Hailey! Squeeze my juices out of me! That's it thrust backward. FUCK! YES! Keep that pace! Let me hear you, baby!"

The harder he thrusts, the louder Hailey moans, and the wetter my dick gets.

"DORIAN! It's clinching so tight! It feels so good! What do I do? What does this mean? FUCK!"

Fuck is right!

I am just as close as Hailey is.

"Just breathe! I t means you're almost ready to orgasm, that's exactly what we want. I am close, too, baby. Keep thrusting your ass towards me! Harder! Faster! FUCK! Keep that pace, baby! We will come together. I can feel you! I can't get enough!"

Me either!

I am right on the edge!

Her innocence is intoxicating!

Hailey keeps pounding her ass against his dick.

"CAPO!"

"I got you, baby! Relax. Let it fill your senses! Fuck I can't hold it back, baby!"

"YES, CAPO! COME! FUCK! IT FEELS SO GOOD! DORIAN!"

Dorian slams into her harder and harder until...

"FUCK YES!!"

FUCK YES!

My whole hand is covered in my come.

Hailey collapses onto the desks, and Dorian collapses on top of her.

He bites her ear, "What do you think, baby? Did I make it worth it? Any regrets?"

They both are panting.

Hailey reaches up and rubs his head, "I think we need to do that again real soon! Worth every fucking second! One regret, though."

Dorian huffs, "What do you regret?"

Hailey giggles, "That I didn't let Crazy Capo deflower me sooner."

Gross!

I cut the feed; I don't want to hear anymore.

At least I got to see hailey naked, at least I got my rocks off.

The next time I see her naked is when I take her precious Capo from her!

I will take her.

I will end both Massimo and Dorian.

It's time to set my plan in motion.

I hacked Toree's phone and fired off a text to Kass.

It reads:
They are together, but the club is falling apart. Dorian isn't in control of Paul. Paul thinks this is his club. You need to come soon.

Sorry, Paul.

You knew better to trust your old man.

16

Euphoria

*D*orian

I pull out and flip Hailey around.

I lick her neck, then grab the back of her head and make her really see me.

"Past the point of no return."

I smash my lips to hers.

Her body relaxes instantly.

In my arms is where she belongs.

She giggles, "Keep your hand at the level of your eye. I forgot you watched that with me and Kass."

My lips move to her neck again.

"Baby, I forget nothing about you. Every movie, every snack, every adventure, and even every meltdown. You were the highlight of my days, now you will be the highlight of my forever."

She licks my cheek, "GRRR, Mine!"

I smile, "Always."

17

Neglect

H^{*ailey*}

Four months later...

YOU HAVE GOT TO BE FUCKING KIDDING ME!

Work has been a nightmare these last few months.

First, after I gave my virginity to Dorian, I got punished big time!

Master was not happy!

He paddled me until I couldn't sit for an entire week!

He said because I was under his direction, I needed to ask permission first, but I didn't.

I regret nothing.

Secondly, Paul has been a real grouch for the last few months.

I know he is running around crazy, but he should still be nice to us.

Third, Dorian has disappeared!

He didn't say goodbye again; he has now been gone for three months.

I am pissed!

Finally fifth, you have got to be fucking kidding me I just took a pregnantcy test!

I AM PREGNANT!

What am I going to do?

I am going to keep working and take care of me and the baby.

I might go back to Chicago.

I won't make any decisions right now; I'll sleep on it.

Fuck you, Dorian!

You left me again.

Fuck you, Master!

Where are you?

Master left me a note saying he needed to step away, but we could pick up when he gets back.

Screw men!

I don't need them!

I am the Ballentine Princess.

You don't fuck with me and live to tell the tale.

18

Missing Part of Me

D^{*orian*}

I have been back in Chicago for the last four months.

Massimo and Kass needed a vacation, so I stayed with the baby so they could enjoy their free time.

They were only gone for two weeks, and as soon as they got back, all hell broke loose.

Someone tried to hack Ballentine Industries' mainframe.

So here I am, scanning every nook and cranny 24/7 to ensure we are clear.

I have been texting Hailey constantly but my messages won't send.

Kass has been checking on her, so I know she is okay, but I hope she isn't pissed at me.

As soon as I solve this disaster, I will return to my Queen!

I need her.

I crave her.

I want to touch her.

I want to hold her.

I need to hear her voice.

I need my heart to be back in my chest.

I need love.

I need passion.

I need trust.

I need her reassurance.

I need to be babied.

I need to feel needed.

I need Hailey!

Past the point of no return...

19

Plan of Action

G*host*

Dorian has been gone for four months, and with the bug I planted in the Ballentine Industries system, he will be gone for at least another month.

Hailey is mine.

I have been in the club every night.

Hailey and I have been growing closer and closer.

She has started to open up to me.

Some of the things she has said make me want to kill Dorian all the more.

She's in love with him.

But not for long; his death will be my final act against the Ballentine Bratva.

I will dismember anyone who gets in the way of my happiness!

My happiness is between Hailey's legs.

20

To The Rescue

Massimo

"Kass, you have got to be fucking joking!"

I hate raising my voice at her, but this was called for!

"It's not a big deal, baby."

I growl, "I am about to bend you over my knee and spank some sense into you! He fucked my sister, and you let him hop on a plane back to her! What the fuck? Dorian is not good enough for her! No one is!"

"BOSSMAN, CALM DOWN!"

Did she just yell at me?!

I snatch her off the counter and drag her to the couch.

I lay her across my lap, "Count!"

"Not this shit aga.."

SMACK

"DAMN YOU! ONE!"

SMACK

"TWO!"

SMACK

"THREE!"

SMACK

"FOUR!"

SMACK

"FIVE, DAMN IT!"

I caress her ass, "Are you done being a brat?"

She nods.

"Tell me everything, Kass! Don't leave anything out! Don't forget any details because I want to murder Dorian right now!"

She turns in my lap and wraps her legs around my torso.

"Baby, you already smacked my ass, so promise me that no matter what I say right now, you won't smack it again?"

Well, that tells me she is guilty.

"I promise, love."

She huffs, "This was all my idea. Hailey came to me and asked to be free from your reign to explore who she wanted to be and have a chance at love. I sent her to Kastaways, not because I needed her. She was tired of you breathing down her neck and not letting her date. I knew that Dorian and Hailey had been crushing on each other for years, and you recently put him in charge of the Bratva expansion in Gulfport. So it was the most logical thing to do: push them together and see what happens. But it got complicated because he had been here, and she just found out she was pregnant. The worst part is that Jared helped find out who hacked our mainframe. It was Harry Ruiz, Paul's dad, who had been spotted at my club. I did some digging. Harry was who your dad had originally sold Hailey to, so get up, Bossman! We have our sister to save and a monster to eliminate."

WHAT THE FUCK!

"KASS! WHAT DID YOU DO?"

She smirks, "I gave her the freedom she wanted! He loves her, and I am sure she loves him, and this baby is a Ballentine blessing. Let's get Sara and Jared to watch the baby, and we will take care of Harry and Paul."

I grumble, "Damn right, we will! And you are not allowed to meddle in anyone else's love life! I can't believe Hailey is pregnant."

She giggles, "Believe it, bossman! You're going to be an uncle!"

I just kiss her cheek.

I am allowed to be mad!

My baby sister is in danger and pregnant by my Capo...

Fuck this!

I'm drinking on the plane ride.

21

Reunited

*D*orian

There she is.

Gorgeous.

Glowing.

She is working her ass off.

She is talking to someone at the bar.

Why did she just caress his hand?

I quickly text Toree to get her to have Hailey meet Master in the dungeon.

It's time she knows the truth.

It's time she knows who she belongs to.

Reunited, and it might feel good, or it might just bite.

Past the point of no return...

2 2

The Truth Comes to Light

H^{*ailey*}

"Hailey, Master wants you in the dungeon in ten minutes. You better hurry."

I look at Toree with a stunned expression, "He's back? What the hell."

She just shrugs, "Give him hell!"

I wink at her, "He will get everything he deserves."

I look at Harry, "Thanks for the company, Harry. I will see you later. Toree will get you anything else you need. Have a great night."

Before I turn, Harry grabs my wrist.

"Be careful, princess. Ghosts lurk in the dark."

I snatch my arm back.

I do not respond to threats or stupidity.

I just nod and head to the elevator.

I will get the answers I am looking for tonight.

The elevator descends; it is time to face the Master.

As the doors open, I hear that sexy whisper.

"I missed you, princess."

Here we go!

"Did you? I don't think you did. I will not be taking my clothes off or following your orders. You will tell me everything I want to know. First question: how long have you been part of the Ballentine Bratva?"

"Fine, princess. I'll play your game. I have been with the Bratva forever."

He dropped the paddle.

"I doubt that's the truth, Master. Second question: when did you get back?"

He sighs, "Twenty minutes ago."

WHAT?

He leans up against the cold, dark dungeon wall.

Why does he have to be so damn sexy?

"Interesting. Third question: where did you go?"

He shifts his weight, "Chicago."

The plot thickens.

"Fourth question: how do you know Dorian? You know too many things he knows."

He gulps.

"Next question, princess."

Avoidance is a nice strategy.

I snicker, "Nope, you don't get any skips. Answer the question."

He removes himself from the wall.

"I'll give you a hint." He removes his shirt, "Every time we play, I use scar tape to cover my Bratva date. Do you want to see my date, princess?"

Why am I nervous?

"Show me! No more lies, Master."

He slowly peels the scar tape from his bicep.

So far, no numbers.

Is he that new to our world?

He stops peeling from the left and starts peeling from the right.

Still no numbers!

What the hell?

Who is this guy?

He stops peeling, and his voice rises from whispering to an even tone.

"Think of me fondly."

A phantom quote?!

NO!

NO!

NO!

"NO! NO WAY!"

I start backing away.

He peels the rest of the tape away.

There it is!

The infinity symbol!

He starts inching toward me.

He backs me up against the wall.

He traps me with his hand on both sides of my face.

He roars, "Do it! Remove my mask! See the truth. See who has always been your precious Master."

My heart is palpitating out of my chest.

My hand slowly moves to his mask.

My hand is shaking.

It can't be him!

I snatch the mask from his face.

Staring back at me is the only man I ever loved, his familiar features now shadowed with betrayal.

The warmth of his smile has turned cold, a reminder of the trust he shattered.

Memories flood my mind—moments filled with laughter now tainted by the deception he wove so effortlessly.

Once the source of my happiness, he walked away again, leaving a void that echoes with unanswered questions and lingering heartache.

I no longer know who the real Dorian is.

All the doubts are swarming my brain, panic is setting in.

I won't be a victim again!

Breathe in, breathe out.

I smack him across the face.

I roar, "You're a monster! You tricked me! You played with my emotions. I fell in love with you, Dorian. But I had doubts because of the master dynamic, I am hurt. You left me again! You didn't contact me; you left me wondering if you would ever return! I gave you my damn virginity, and you punished me for it! How fucked up is that?"

His hands droop to his side.

He looks defeated.

GOOD!

"Put your shirt on, Dorian. We are done. I will work all my shifts for the rest of the week before returning to Chicago. If Massimo didn't assign you here permanently, I will ensure he does now. I never want to see you again."

Disappear, Dorian.

Hide in the darkness.

We don't need you.

23

Goodbye for Now

D^{orian}

Just as I feared, Hailey hates me.

She feels betrayed and lied to.

But she loves me!

I will fix this.

"Please, don't walk away from me, princess. My heart feels so empty without your light. I see a future for us, filled with laughter and love, where we can share our dreams together. Don't close the door on what we have! Allow me to show you the depth of my love!"

She snaps, "NEVER! I trusted you! You shattered my trust and my heart! Oh, by the way, when you left, I discovered I am pregnant. I'll give one guess whose it is! I DON'T NEED YOU!"

PREGNANT!

Speechless.

Never have I considered children.

Hailey is carrying our child?!

I drop to the floor.

I don't know what to do.

Am I ready for this?

Hailey must take my silence negatively.

"Goodbye, Master."

Gone like the wind, she doesn't look back.

24

Now is MY Chance

*H*arry *(Ghost)*

Hailey is storming out of the club.

She looks distraught and confused.

Looks like Dorian did all the hard work for me.

Hailey dropped her phone on the concrete.

"Here, I will get it for you."

She looks up at me with those sad eyes.

"Hey Harry, thank you. I'm not going back to work tonight. Sorry if I ruined your night."

Oh, sweetheart, I am about to ruin you!

"You didn't ruin my night, love. Let's go to dinner to cheer you up."

Her stomach growled as soon as dinner left my lips.

Trust me, baby girl, that's my hunger for you.

"Sure, that sounds great, thank you."

Time to disappear!

25

My Sister's Guard

M^{assimo}

We arrive in Gulfport, Mississippi, and the difference between Chicago and the South is evident.

The air is cleaner here in Mississippi.

The hospitality is its best attribute.

Kass wanted this club to be another source of income for her and a place for some of the girls to work.

It doesn't hurt that we get to use the amenities; we have our pick of all of the playrooms.

But we aren't here to play!

We are here to bring my sister home!

I am mainly here to decide if Dorian should be a part of this family any longer.

He betrayed me.

He has been my brother since before Hailey was born; he was also supposed to be her protector.

I am conflicted.

He's been a major part of my life.

Is it time to cut the cord?

Is it time to burn the infinity symbol off his bicep?

We finally arrive at Kastaways; I head straight for the second floor.

I'm taking the secret passage to the dungeon.

I don't want him to know I am here yet.

Dorian better hope Kass stays by my side, or the Bratva Monster will arrive.

26

Bratva Monster

D^{orian}

I made it to level two after changing out of my master facade.

I slide onto the bar stool.

"You really fucked up, didn't you, boss?" Toree says as she slides a whiskey my way.

I stare into the glass before downing it.

"Yes, I did, Tore. I love her. Now, she hates me even though she's having my baby. She says she's leaving after this week, and she never wants to see me again. I don't blame her. I hope she forgives me. How could today get any worse?"

Toree sighs, "It did get worse. Someone triggered the secret passage to the dungeon, so you're needed down there. I know who triggered it, but I cannot say anything."

Fantastic, just where I need to go back to the place where I broke her heart.

Toree scoots me another whiskey.

I down the whiskey in two seconds flat.

I nod at Toree.

Hopefully, whoever tripped the passage is ready for a fight.

I am ready to destress.

As I make it into the dungeon, I flip the light switch.

Not even a flicker.

I reach for my phone to flip the breaker; I hear shuffling.

"Show yourself! Show yourself now, and you won't get hurt!"

The next thing I know, there's a cynical laugh next to my ear.

"You couldn't hurt me if you tried! You brought the monster back!"

FUCK!

The monster has been hidden for years!

He was docile; what could have triggered the Monster?

OH FUCK!

HE KNOWS!

"WAIT! I DIDN..."

That's the last thing I say before I crumble to the ground in agony; the monster knows precisely where to hit to make my world go black.

27

Darkness

H^{ailey}

Darkness is all around.

My eyes feel heavy and stubbornly refuse to open.

A suffocating darkness envelops me, and a dull throbbing pain pulses at my temples.

What on earth happened?

The last clear memory I have is of sharing a cozy dinner with Harry, the laughter and conversation fading into an unsettling void.

Stay calm.

I remind myself not to let panic squeeze my chest.

I am not a victim.

I need to take stock of my surroundings.

I soon realize that my hands are tightly bound, as are my feet, restricting my movement.

Yet, beneath me, something soft cradles my body, and I sense the warmth of a cover draped over me, adding to the disorienting atmosphere.

Even though I strain to see, a heavy blindfold obscures my vision, further deepening my sense of dread.

Do not panic.

Breathe in, breathe out, breathe in, breathe out.

Protect yourself and protect your baby; never give up, keep fighting.

You have people who need you and care about you, so you're not a waste of space.

Panic attacks have always been a big problem for me.

Kass gave me some tricks and tips on how to fix them as long as I concentrate on everything but the panic attack I will be fine, or if I eat something sour but I don't have anything sour with me.

That's why I have a stash of sour candy in my purse, but my purse is in my locker at the club.

I thought all the people that wanted to harm me were dead.

I thought my life would be normal and safe without my dad around.

Who would want to capture me?

Big Brother has always kept me safe.

A small part of me thought Dorian would be my protector too, but I guess he really doesn't care about me.

I trusted the wrong person; I fell in love with the wrong person.

From now on, I will get guidance from the people around me instead of making my own decisions.

Once I get out of here, I will focus on just me and the baby.

I will never put anything over myself or my child.

Suddenly, I hear locks click.

Then an eerie voice speaks, "Beautiful, just beautiful. I have you right where I want you, where you should have been 10 years ago. When your father sold you to me."

WHAT THE FUCK?

"Who are you? Everyone who was a part of Dad's deal is dead!"

His haunting laugh hangs in the air, "Everyone that got caught is dead; I used a fake name. Back then, I was known as Ghost because I was only found when I wanted to be found. Now, I go by my real name because I'm old and lazy. But I was conniving enough to trick you, little girl. I was so tired of using the sweet and caring persona! I was there to gain your trust so you would be mine finally after ten long years."

Conniving?

An act?

Nice?

Caring?

Slimmy, sweaty hands caress my face.

The blindfold slowly comes untied, and it slides down my chest.

"Happy to see me, baby girl.?"

I gasp, "Harry, what the hell? What do you want from me?"

28

Too Much Truth

H^{*arry*}

Hailey's face tells me everything I need to know.

"What? You're not happy to see me? I gave you a place to stay that's better than your shitty apartment. The Bratva really makes their members slum it these days. Whether you like it or not, you are mine! You were sold to me ten years ago. I can do anything I want to you, and no one can stop me. Want to know a secret, baby girl?"

She gags, "Stop calling me that! I don't care what arrangement you had with my Dad that is over! I am my own person, and you are a sick monster! I will never be yours!"

My cruel laugh echoes, "I have seen how you fuck. He was not good enough for you, but I am."

She looks disgusted and hurt.

Oh well!

There is a syringe in my back pocket.

I am going to drug her so I can get what is rightfully mine, but only if I need to.

"We can do this the easy way or the hard way, baby girl. Make your choice."

Tears flow from her eyes,"I am not a victim. But I know when I have lost. I will do whatever you say, Harry."

I caress her cheek, "Good girl. I'll start with your mouth."

I unzip my pants and free my cock.

I have waited ten years for this.

This is going to be heaven.

"Open wide, baby girl. I will pleasure you as long as you follow my orders. I don't do well with disobedient slaves. Be good to me and I'll always be good to you. That is my only rule."

I slowly inch my cock into her waiting mouth.

My wildest dream is becoming a reality.

No more watching her on a screen.

Now I can touch her!

29

Punishment For the Master

Massimo

Before Dorian awakes, I tie him to the cross.

He did this to himself.

Nobody defiles the Bratva Princess!

No one is allowed to undermine my trust and escape the consequences!

I hold loyalty in high regard, and anyone who dares to betray it will face repercussions they won't forget.

Should I let him sleep?

Nope!

No mercy!

I grab the bucket of ice water and toss it over his limp body; he jerks awake.

"Hello, asshole. Ready for your punishment? I don't care if you aren't! You fucked up, so now you will find out first-hand what happens to those who betray the Monster!"

Realization hits his eyes, "Please, boss! Please don't kill me. I have always been loyal to you; we have been through it all! I am so sorry!"

I flick open my knife and inch toward him.

"You were supposed to protect her, not defile her!"

"Listen, boss. It's not what.."

"I SHOULD CUT OFF YOUR DICK! YOU DON'T DE-SERVE TO USE IT OR EVEN HOLD IT!"

I inch toward him and press my knife to his crotch.

Tears stream from his eyes, "Please, boss! I LOVE HER!"

"You love her? Since when? The animosity between you has been going on for years! I should remove you from the Bratva! My sister Dorian? You could've had any woman you wanted; why her?"

"BOSS! I LOVED HER SINCE THE FIRST TIME SHE KICKED ME!"

WHAT???

My anger is waning.

I close my knife.

Are his intentions true?

"Dorian, you have loved her for twelve years? Why did you tell me? Do you not trust me? I am not always a monster. If your love is true, I would never stop y'all from being together."

Dorian finally looks me in the eyes, "I love her more than breath itself. I'm past the point of no return."

I cut Dorian free from the cross; he plummets to the icy floor.

"Then you are still my brother, but you better make it official."

He chuckles, "I'll take her to the chapel next time she is here."

I pat him on the back, "Punishment complete. Let's go get a drink."

We head up to level two; as soon as we get there, Toree screams across the bar.

"CODE RED! HAILEY HAS BEEN TAKEN BY GHOST!"

30

Missing Hailey

D^{orian}

Massimo's voice roars, "I AM SO FUCKING TIRED OF CODE REDS! EVERYONE OUT! WE ARE CLOSED AS OF NOW!"

All the patrons exit without a word.

Most of those who attend the club know all or some about our world.

We head up to the top level to strategize.

Kass speaks first: "Toree reviewed everything; it was Harry who took her. Dorian, Paul has been executed. Harry is Paul's father, and Paul has been working with him all along, even giving him access to the club's mainframe. I do not tolerate vital mistakes. I tracked Hailey; she's at Harry's condo. Dorian, we will set you up on the app with Hailey's tracking information; she opted for the tracker to be implanted. We can easily get in since he doesn't realize I own the building. It's condo 4A. The key will be waiting for us at the front desk. Let's go get our girl back!"

"Let's not waste any more time! If he harms her, I will end him!" Massimo cries.

"I am ending him no matter what! He touched my woman! Touch her, and you sign your death wish!"

Massimo and Kass just nod.

I'm coming for you, Hailey.

I will no longer treat you like a feeble princess; I'm ready to claim you as my queen.

31

Bite Marks

H^{ailey}

HE IS REALLY ABOUT TO PUT HIS DICK IN MY MOUTH!

His little wrinkly dick is staring at me.

Dorian's is four times his size!

I can't let Harry take advantage of me!

He is inching towards my mouth with it.

What do I do?

Do I just let it happen?

NO, FUCK THAT!

THINK HAILEY!?!

I got it!

I gag at the sweaty taste as he shoves it on my tongue.

He shoves it further down my throat, "Take it like the trash you are!"

That was the last straw!

I muster all the strength I have.

I shove all my weight forward.

Before Harry can react, I lock my jaw around his dick.

I bite down with all my strength; he deserves it to be bit off!

His screams radiate around the condo, "You, bitch! Release my dick before I kill you!"

He is thrashing and moving.

I want to puke just because of how he tastes.

He thrashes so much he throws us on the floor; that's all it took.

He thrashed so hard it caused me to bite down with full force.

Blood pours into my mouth.

Harry rolls around on the floor, holding his nonexistent penis.

I spit his dick on the floor and reach for his discarded knife and syringe.

I plunge the syringe into his neck.

"Night night asshole! My face will be the last one you see!"

Panic overcomes his features.

I slit his throat from ear to ear.

"NO ONE MESSES WITH THE BRATVA PRINCESS AND LIVES TO TELL THE TALE!"

32

Scared but in Love

D^{orian}

Before we open the door, Hailey screams.

"NO ONE MESSES WITH THE BRATVA PRINCESS AND LIVES TO TELL THE TALE!"

Oh shit!

I get the door open as quickly as I can!

I don't know what I was expecting to see, but I was not prepared for this!

Then, a stench of iron is strong in the air; blood coats the entire floor.

It looks like Harry bled out.

What is that worm-like thing on the floor?

I look at Hailey, "Princess, are you okay?"

She's covered in blood from her mouth to her neck.

The bloody knife clatters to the floor.

She looks me in the eye, "You couldn't have showed up ten minutes earlier? Before I bit his dick off!?"

EXCUSE ME!

"YOU DIDN'T. I think I am going to be sick." Massimo turns green.

Kass giggles, "That's badass! But why did you bite it off and slit his throat?"

Hailey grabbed a tissue from the bedside table and cleaned her face, "He forced his wormy dick in my mouth, so I bit it off. I slit his throat because he didn't deserve to live after attacking me."

I don't know if I should be scared or turned on.

I think I am both.

Massimo speaks, "I have a cleaning crew on the way, and they will be here in five minutes. Let's head back to the club to sort this all out."

I nod.

Kass drapes her arm around Hailey.

My love is safe, both of them.

33

Epilogue- From Princess to Queen

*H*ailey

ONE YEAR LATER..

Here we are, living life the best we can.

I am no longer Hailey Ballentine.

Three hundred and sixty-two days ago, I got married.

I am now Hailey Petrov.

We live here in Gulfport, Mississippi.

Massimo put us both in charge of his new Bratva crew on the Gulf Coast.

Crime has gone down fifty percent in just one year.

I made Big Brother proud, I showed him I can reign on my own.

But Massimo and Kass still call once a week to check on me, Dorian, and our twins.

That's right, we were blessed with twin girls, Savannah and Dawn.

I now reign over the Gulf Coast.

But most of all, I reign over Dorian.

I am his Queen.

I have earned my crown!

One day, my girls will not settle until their man conquers the world!

There is a King or Queen for everyone; you just have to find them!

In the end, happiness reigns over all.

THE END..... FOR NOW

34

Extended Epilogue

Toree

I love my job at Kastways.

I love all the extra stuff I get to learn, too.

I have learned how to control situations to my advantage by using my assets.

I have learned that I deserve love!

I have learned that I have a small kink.

I have come to realize that genuine love is increasingly hard to find in today's world, where meaningful connections seem to be overshadowed by the fast pace of life.

I know the not-so-legal Bratva world exists, and I am fine with that.

Working for them is a blessing and a curse.

I just want my chance at love, a chance to thrive.

Why is my chance at love constantly drifting away?

Am I that repulsive?

Will my chance come?

Or will my chance be frightened off by Kastaways?

Or will I be cast away?

Chances can come once in a lifetime.

Or the only chance you need can hit you out of nowhere.

Which chance will be mine?

About the Author

AUTHOR SUMMER N DAWN IS A SMALL-TOWN WOMAN TRYING TO LIVE HER DREAM.

SHE HAS CEREBRAL PALSY BUT DOESN'T LET THAT STOP HER. SHE CREATES WORLDS SO EVERYONE CAN FIND A PLACE TO FIT IN.

www.ingramcontent.com/pod-product-compliance
Ingram Content Group UK Ltd.
Pitfield, Milton Keynes, MK11 3LW, UK
UKHW032334131224
452011UK00004B/42